EXPLORE MICHIGAN

MACKINAC

George Cantor has been a journalist in the Detroit area for more than 40 years. He worked for the *Detroit Free Press* and the *Detroit News* as a baseball writer, travel writer, reporter and columnist.

His proudest achievements were covering the 1968 Detroit Tigers in their championship season, raising two beautiful daughters and seeing columns he had written years ago still hanging on refrigerator doors around the state.

He also has written 15 books on sports, travel and history.

George and his wife Sherry are residents of West Bloomfield, along with their irascible west highland terrier, Charlie.

EXPLORE MICHIGAN

MACKINAC

An Insider's Guide to Michigan

George Cantor

The University of Michigan Press
Ann Arbor
&
Petoskey Publishing Company
Traverse City

Published in the United States of America by
The University of Michigan Press
Manufactured in the United States of America
Printed on acid-free paper

2008   2007   2006   2005   4   3   2   1

ISBN 0-472-03111-2

Library of Congress Cataloging-in-publication Data on File

Explore Michigan:
Mackinac was reviewed by
Terry Phipps, ten years the official
photographer of Mackinac Island

Cover photograph provided by
Marge Beaver, Photography Plus
www.photography-plus.com

Inside photography courtesy of
Terry Phipps, photographer of
Seasons of Sleeping Bear and
Seasons of Little Traverse Bay,
phipps@gtii.com

CONTENTS

Explore Michigan: An Insider's Guide to Michigan is not meant to be a complete listing of every restaurant or every shop; it is truly meant to be an "insider's" guide. It recommends the places that the locals, and in the case of the tourist areas, long-time summer residents, know about, frequent and recommend to their family and friends.

For example, in Traverse City, the parking meters have a button that you can hit for thirty free minutes. In Leelanau County, the National Park Service conducts winter snowshoe tours of the park. In Detroit, there are cozy restaurants that out-of-towners rarely find. And if you want a more affordable, and quiet weekend at the Grand Hotel on Mackinac Island, it is now open in early spring.

Author George Cantor has been writing travel books for over twenty years. A life-long Michigander, he has traveled and explored Michigan with the gusto it takes to make these books special. Though they are guidebooks, they make for a good read before, during and after you plan to visit. George also wanted to make sure that he really had the local flare for each book in this series, so he agreed to have locals review each book and give their comments to him.

The result is *Explore Michigan: An Insider's Guide to Michigan*, where the aerial photographs on the covers by exceptionally talented Marge Beaver invite you in. Once you start reading, you are on your way to invaluable information that puts you on the inside of what our great state has to offer.

--the publishers

STRAITS OF MACKINAC

The Top Ten Don't Miss List

1. Take a carriage ride around the island.
2. Even better, rent a bike and pedal around it.
3. Have some fudge.
4. Visit Fort Mackinac up on the hill above town.
5. Walk through the historic buildings on Market Street.
6. Take in the view from the parks on the Mackinaw City and St. Ignace sides of the Mackinac Bridge.
7. Take the kids to the Butterfly House.
8. Pay your respects to Father Marquette at the site of his mission in St. Ignace.
9. Walk up to the Grand Hotel.
10. Find an empty lawn chair at Mission Point and watch the world go by.

MACKINAC ISLAND

A beautiful view flying in

"But it's kitsch," said the wife of the professor of architecture.

"No, it's not," argued her husband. "If it's genuine, it can't be kitsch."

We were sitting on the terrace of the Iroquois Hotel; enjoying a whitefish lunch, admiring the view across the Straits of Mackinac and eavesdropping on the conversation at the next table.

"Well, in my opinion," she said, "it still looks like Disneyland."

She had a point. Mackinac Island is just too perfect---if you're willing to overlook the fragrant horse deposits that decorate its streets.

Entering the town from the ferry dock, it looks as if it had been put together by a set designer trying for a Michigan version of Brigadoon.

The rows of white buildings. The horse-drawn wagons, or drays as they are called here. The bicycle traffic jams. All of it lifted whole from another time, another century and deposited on an island where every view suggests a post-card. Mackinac has been called "the Bermuda of the North" and that's not too far off the mark.

No wonder the cult movie "Somewhere in Time," about a modern man traveling back to a different era to find the love he had lost, was set here.

There is also little wonder why Mackinac Island has been one of America's favorite resorts since the 1870s. For all intents and purposes, it may still be the 1870s here. No motorized vehicles (except those used for emergencies). Erratic cell phone reception. When the weather turns bad in winter it can be cut off from the mainland for days at a time. The Great Lakes supply the air conditioning.

Not a bad time to be caught in.

Most visitors get their first view of it from the deck of one of the ferries from Mackinaw City, at the tip of the Lower Peninsula.

To the Native Americans who gave it a name, the island's outline suggested a great turtle, and it was a place of truce, worship and trade. You may be hard pressed to discern the turtle as you approach the island, but you will feel the same sense of awe that brought the tribes here for centuries.

The name is probably Ojibwa in origin and was pronounced with the final 'c' clicked off. Mack-in-ack. Even the French, who are usually quite willing to ignore such consonants, said it that way.

But when the British took over the Straits area in the 1760s they decided, as only the British can, that it should properly be called Mackinaw. That's why the mainland city is spelled the way it is and why the same pronunciation extends to the island, even though it is still spelled Mackinac.

Confused? History can do that to you.

When the French began exploring the interior of North America, this was the first part of Michigan they reached. You can see why by looking at a map. The most direct and easiest water route west from Montreal was to follow the Ottawa and French rivers to Georgian Bay, then on to Lake Huron and the Straits.

Etienne Brule was probably the first European to see Mackinac Island, sometime around 1620. Not until the

Jesuits arrived, however, was there a permanent French presence. Father Jacques Marquette, a vigorous mix of missionary and explorer, established a church at Sault Ste. Marie in 1668. Three years later, he came to St. Ignace and founded the first mission on the Straits.

By this time, news of other riches had made it back to Quebec. An inexhaustible supply of beaver fur, a fashion staple in Europe, was to be found here. In 1670, the Hudson's Bay Company was organized in England to exploit this resource, and within a few years French and British traders were in competition throughout the Northern Great Lakes and beyond.

Fort Michilimackinac, on the present site of Mackinaw City, was built by France in 1715 and became a huge trading center. The fort was the rendezvous point for voyageurs, trappers who brought in a season's worth of pelts for transport to Quebec and Europe. In return, they received the trade goods they needed for their Indian customers to obtain more furs.

Within a generation, competition for this trade, among other issues, had placed France and England on a collision course. When it came, the French and Indian War shifted political and economic control of the area to the British--- although much of the fur trade still was carried on by French trappers.

France's Indian allies refused to accept the result of the war, however, and in 1763 they rose up in Pontiac's Rebellion. The British garrison at Michilimackinac was slaughtered. While the uprising ultimately failed, England began to wonder about its ability to defend this fort if war should come again.

So when the Revolutionary War began going badly for Britain in the west, the fort's commandant, Patrick Sinclair, decided to move the garrison to Mackinac Island. Equipment and entire buildings were dragged across the frozen Straits during the winter of 1779-80, and by summer Fort Mackinac was completed.

The attack Sinclair feared never came. Under the treaty

A step back in time

that ended the war, however, the island had to be surrendered
to the Americans anyhow. The British fur traders were outraged. They understood the critical importance of the island.

So did an entrepreneur in faraway New York City. John
Jacob Astor saw that the way now was open for Americans
to take control of this lucrative business. In 1806 he char-
tered the American Fur Co., with headquarters on the
island. British traders were given commercial rights but they
were none too happy with the emerging American domi-
nance. They wanted Mackinac back.

When war broke out again, in 1812, a surprise British
landing on the far side of the island from the well-defended
fort quickly recaptured it. But the triumph was brief.
Mackinac was restored to American control with this
treaty, too, and British traders permanently excluded.

Given a clear hand, Astor built his company into the
foundation of one of the great American fortunes. His
agents soon controlled 95 percent of the fur trade in the
Great Lakes from their base at Mackinac.

But the fur era was coming to a close. The ever astute

Astor realized that fashions were changing and in 1834 he sold his interest in the company. Within a decade, the trade had shifted to the Pacific Northwest, and Mackinac Island began to decline as a commercial center.

The emphasis shifted to fishing for a time and many of the former fur depots were converted to storage icehouses. But by 1840, a more lasting change had arrived. Regular steamboat service brought visitors to Mackinac and they liked what they saw.

"The climate during the summer months is delightful," wrote the poet and influential journalist William Cullen Bryant. "There is no air more pure and elastic."

Adventuresome travelers from the East were intrigued by the Native American culture on the island---much as succeeding generations would be fascinated by the tribes of the Southwest when rail travel opened that area. The scenery sent them into rhapsodies of praise.

In 1875 the island was made a national park, the second after Yellowstone. But 20 years later, it was transferred to Michigan's control and became the first of its state parks.

Large scale tourism had been established with the prosperity that followed the Civil War. Regularly scheduled ferry service on the Arnold Line (still in operation) began in 1878. Trains arrived in Mackinaw City and waiting carriages took passengers right to the dock.

The Island House, oldest operating hotel on the island, opened in 1852. But it remained for the Grand Hotel to turn Mackinac into a famous destination.

Built as a railroad promotion in 1887, the Grand targeted the social elite of Chicago, Detroit and other Midwestern cities. With its 628-foot long, pillared front porch overlooking the Straits, its sunken gardens and luxurious amenities, the hotel quickly established itself as a preferred summer rendezvous for the privileged.

The most important decision about Mackinac, however, may have been made in 1896. That's when all motorized vehicles were banned. It was done for the most basic economic reason. Drivers of the island's carriages did not want any future competition from the "horseless" variety that was just starting to find a market among the wealthy sporting set. The dray drivers were well organized and a strong political force on the island, so their concerns prevailed.

The wisdom of that choice is apparent from the moment you set foot on Mackinac. Michigan is the same state that gave the world the Motor City. But on Mackinac, you get around by foot, by hoof or by bicycle. It is one of the qualities that make the island so appealing...and so different.

It may also be why fashionable resorts come and go, but Mackinac remains a steady star.

The best advice is to stay overnight. Because only when the day-trippers depart on the last ferry to the mainland, and the peace of another era descends on the island, does Mackinac's magic stand fully revealed.

THE TOWNS

Mackinac. At last count, there were 523 people living on the island year-round. To them, you are known as a fudgie----which is sort of the Mackinac equivalent to a Floridian calling you a snowbird. Still, there are worse things with which to be identified than candy.

Despite the 3,500 tourists a day who flock here in summer, and the small army of temporary workers who supply services for them, Mackinac is essentially a small town. There are police and fire departments, a school, a medical center. Taxes are collected. The usual small town stuff. The difference is that most land is held on leases going back to late 18th Century land grants, and the biggest property owner is the State of Michigan. It has title to 1,700 acres of the 2,200 on the island.

State regulations cover every proposed external change to buildings. That perfect Victorian appearance isn't sustained by accident.

The island pretty much shuts down between November and early May. During the depth of winter, shopping trips to the mainland must be meticulously planned in advance. The sudden onset of weather, which happens a lot, can change everything, and people do get stranded for a day or two.

But look at it this way. Things like car insurance, shoveling out the driveway and 45 minute commutes to work are merely rumors. Mackinac residents will take the tradeoff.

Mackinaw City. Most travelers will make the trip to the island from this town, on I-75 at the tip of the Lower Peninsula. It is barely larger than Mackinac in population, with fewer than 900 residents, and exists pretty much as an appendage of the island tourist trade.

There is a heavy concentration of motels near the ferry docks, with rates somewhat lower than what you'll find on the island. Souvenir stores and eating places cluster thickly along Central and Huron avenues. There is even a fair-sized mall, Mackinaw Crossings, near the intersection of those two thoroughfares.

The reconstructed Fort Michilimackinac is the main attraction, but there are also wonderful views of the bridge and island from the park along Huron Avenue, north of the downtown area.

St. Ignace. If there is a metropolis of the Straits area, this is it. With 2,700 inhabitants the Upper Peninsula town is almost twice the size of the other two communities combined.

There is also ferry service to Mackinac from here and it's a bit less congested than the Mackinaw City side. But you have to make the bridge crossing to get here; which, of course, is not a problem if you intend to go on and tour the UP.

There is more of a residential feel to St. Ignace and its stores actually sell useful items instead of bottle openers shaped like bears. It also has several historic sites associated with Father Marquette and a good Native American museum. Lodging and restaurant choices, however, are more limited than in Mackinaw City.

LOCAL COLOR

Father Jacques Marquette

He came to the Straits of Mackinac in 1671, a Jesuit priest with a lifelong dream to work among the Indians of the New World. The mission he established here was named St. Ignace, for Ignatius Loyola, the founder of his order.

It was the first European settlement in this area. But the 34-year old Marquette was restless to move on, hearing a call for an adventure that he already had come to identify as his life's work. It was a quest that took him on one of the great voyages of discovery in American history.

He was born into a distinguished family at Laon, France and took holy orders at the age of 19. The young priest studied and taught in his homeland, preparing himself for a missionary post in North America.

When it came, in 1666, he quickly set about to make himself fluent in as many Indian dialects as he could master. His special aptitude was the Huron language, and he was sent from Quebec to work among them; first at Sault Ste.

Marie, and then at the western end of Lake Superior, near
what is now Ashland, Wisconsin.

While living there he heard reports of a great river that
rose nearby and flowed to the sea. Marquette was convinced that this was the Northwest Passage to Asia and he
was determined to find it. Before he could act upon that
belief, though, the Huron were attacked by their enemies,
the Dakota, and he had to join them on a retreat to sanctu-
ary in the Mackinac area.

But St. Ignace would be his home for only two years.
Stories of the great river had made it back to Quebec and
an expedition, headed by fur trader Louis Joliet, was being
readied. Friends who knew of Marquette's linguistic skills
convinced Joliet to take him along as an interpreter.

There were seven men who left the mission in May,
1673 and began their voyage into the unknown. Traveling
down Lake Michigan, they found the mouth of the Fox
River, portaged to the Wisconsin River and one month into
the journey became the first Europeans known to have
reached the northern Mississippi River.

Marquette described his reaction as "a joy which I am
unable to make known." There was disappointment, however, when it became apparent that the great river was not
the route to China. It flowed south, not west. But they followed it all the way to Arkansas, then turned back upon
receiving reports of Spanish soldiers ahead.

The expedition opened up the continent's interior to
French traders and, eventually, to settlers. Marquette back-
tracked as far as Green Bay, but the rigors of the voyage
began catching up to him over the next winter. He fell ill
while preaching to tribes in what is now the Chicago area.

Suspecting that the end was approaching, he tried to get
back to St. Ignace in a canoe with two voyageurs. But near
present day Ludington, Michigan. the party had to put
ashore and the 39 year old priest, his body worn out by the
travails of living in the wilderness, passed away. It was two
years almost to the day since he had left the mission.

He was returned to St. Ignace for burial the following

year. But when the mission was abandoned, in 1706, the site of the grave was lost, not to be rediscovered for 171 years. It is now a part of Marquette Mission Park, in the town.

Marquette left his name to cities, rivers, a great university in Milwaukee, and streets all across the Upper Midwest. He is best remembered in this area by the lovely park named for him at the base of Fort Mackinac on Mackinac Island. The statue of him there, in clerical robes, looking boldly out toward the Straits, was unveiled in 1909.

Robert Rogers

To some he was a visionary and adventurer; to others a scoundrel and petty crook. But no other individual is as closely identified with the search for the Northwest Passage as this British military officer, and the Mackinac area was his base.

Leading his company of Rangers on a campaign of guerilla warfare, Rogers' exploits in the French and Indian War made him a heroic figure in England and America. Long after his death he was celebrated as a courageous fighter and adventurer in the best-selling novel, *Northwest Passage*, and portrayed in the 1940 movie version by Spencer Tracy.

The truth, as usual, is a bit more elusive.

Rogers was born in Massachusetts in 1731. When war with France and its Indian allies broke out, he volunteered to assemble a corps of irregulars to take the fight to the enemy. Some historians credit him with originating the ranger tactics of surprise and mobility, hitting the enemy when and where they least expected it. One winter he furnished his men with snowshoes, crossed a frozen lake and destroyed an Indian force.

He won even greater acclaim by breaking Pontiac's siege of Detroit in 1763. He was received in London by King George III and feted by admirers. But the pursuit of the passage had already insinuated itself in his brain and that would be his undoing. The king refused to finance a search for the passage, appointing Major Rogers, instead, as the commandant of Fort Michilimackinac, in Mackinaw City.

When he got here in 1766 he was at the height of his fame. But whether through ambition or arrogance, Rogers was working on his own agenda.

He sent an associate, Jonathan Carver, on an unauthorized search for the passage, which only got as far as Minnesota before having to turn back. But Carver also made trading alliances with several tribes in the lakes area, which seemed to be a part of Rogers' greater plan.

He wanted to turn Michilimackinac into the hub of a vast trade network. During parleys at the fort to gather support from the Indians, he gave out lavish gifts. What his ultimate purpose was has never been ascertained. His record-keeping was sloppy and no one could track his financial dealings.

But to his superiors in the army, it appeared as if he intended to establish an independent fiefdom in the northern lakes and, possibly, forge an alliance with the French in the Mississippi Valley. To make it worse, he was caught engaging in a personal rum trade with the Indians, a practice forbidden by British law.

He was arrested in 1767, charged with treason and put on trial in Montreal. He was acquitted, but the cloud always remained over his reputation.

At the start of the Revolutionary War, he offered his services to George Washington. But his motives were still suspect and he was rebuffed. Rogers, instead, formed a Loyalist raiding force in the New York City area but accomplished little.

He had to leave America after the war, and lived out his life in England, forgotten by those who once had adored him. He died there in obscurity in 1795.

Robert Stuart

The man who built the Mackinac fur trade, John Jacob Astor, never actually set foot on the island. Furs made him a fortune, the first American millionaire. But it was actually his agent on Mackinac, Robert Stuart, who left the more lasting imprint.

Stuart was a rather incredible fellow in his own right.

Born in Scotland in 1785, a descendant of noble chieftains, he emigrated to Canada when he was 22. Astor was spending much of his time in Montreal then, trying to learn as much as he could about the fur trade, which was then controlled by British interests in Canada.

He was impressed by Stuart's ambitions and gave him a place on his historic expedition to Oregon in 1810. This was a perilous sea journey, intended to establish an American trading presence at the mouth of the Columbia River. When the party landed, at the site of present day Astoria, the situation became even more acute when their boat was attacked by Indians and destroyed.

Stranded on the distant shore, Stuart and five others set out to make their way back East overland and get help for their colleagues. Lewis and Clark had made the west-to-east trek a few years before, but far to the north, along the Missouri River. Stuart, instead, followed the Snake and found the route that would soon become the Oregon Trail.

His crowning achievement was becoming the first European known to have crossed Wyoming's South Pass. This was the easiest way through the Rockies, the route of wagon trains and the intercontinental railroad in a few more decades. Stuart finally reached St. Louis, in May, 1813 after nearly a year of incredible hardship.

Astor rewarded his employee by putting him in charge of the Mackinac depot, the center of the American Fur Company trade. He remained there for 15 years, from 1819 to 1834, until Astor sold out for an estimated $20 million.

Stuart never saw that kind of money. But his home on Market Street was the business and social center of the island. He administered the vast Astor empire in the West from this place; receiving furs from more than 2,000 employees and handing out trade goods in return. Visitors to the island were entertained at the house, which still stands.

He made a reputation as a man who was fair to trappers and Indians alike, and after Astor's company was sold he was named Indian agent on the island. Later he became Michigan's state treasurer, before passing away in 1843.

William Beaumont and Alexis St. Martin

The two are forever linked in the annals of medical history, brought together by an accident on Mackinac Island that opened up vast realms of knowledge about the human digestive system.

Beaumont was the post physician at Fort Mackinac. He came from the Lake Champlain area, where he earned his medical license and served as an army doctor in the War of 1812. He entered private practice in Plattsburgh, N.Y., but re-enlisted and was posted to Mackinac in 1819.

St. Martin was a voyageur for the American Fur Company. While on the island, he was accidentally shot in the abdomen. The wound was about the size of the palm of a man's hand and damaged a lung, some ribs and his stomach.

Medical facilities were fairly primitive. Beaumont complained that the hospital, in a former warehouse, was open to snow in winter, rain in summer and smoke almost always. When St. Martin was carried in to his surgery, he patched up the wound as best he could.

It was June, 1822. Beaumont was 37 years old; St. Martin, 11 years younger. For most of the next decade, the two would be a most unlikely couple.

Beaumont managed to heal most of the damage but could never satisfactorily close the wound to the stomach. He left a flap of skin to cover it. But he soon realized that what he had really done was opened a window to the digestive process.

Since St. Martin no longer could work, Beaumont hired him as a handyman. This, apparently, gave implied consent to conduct experiments on his stomach.

The doctor would attach various food items to St. Martin's stomach and then withdraw them to observe the effect of gastric juices over time. The experiments continued for the next nine years, as the two men went on to three different Army posts.

St. Martin would at times get upset over this odd existence and Beaumont took the opportunity to observe the effect of anger on digestion. He left for home in Quebec on one occasion, but returned when Beaumont was transferred to Washington, D.C.

In 1833, Beaumont published his seminal work on "The Physiology of Digestion." It earned him a permanent place in medical science. He later opened a successful practice in St. Louis and died there after a fall on the ice in 1853.

St. Martin lived on for 58 years after his injury. His stomach never fully healed and his family refused to disclose the site of his grave, fearing that body snatchers would dig him up to conduct more experiments. Finally, 82 years after his death, in 1962, the burial site was marked with an historical sign.

Beaumont's work is memorialized in the old American Fur Co. store on Mackinac. One of Michigan's largest hospitals, in the Detroit suburb of Royal Oak, is named for him.

Henry Schoolcraft

The tides of history and fortune brought several remarkable men to Mackinac over the years. Schoolcraft is not as widely known as some, but his influence may have extended further than any of them. He opened a new door in American literature and left dozens of names upon the land.

He was born in New York's Hudson Valley in 1793 and trained as a geologist. As a young man he had gathered valuable information on lead mines in Missouri. So when an expedition was planned in 1820 to the unknown country of the Upper Peninsula, Schoolcraft signed on.

The party crossed the entire UP and tried unsuccessfully to locate the source of the Mississippi River in Minnesota. Schoolcraft saw significant traces of copper and iron, finds that would soon touch off a rush for riches. But he also returned from his voyage with something else; a profound love for the Native American culture he found there.

His career in geology was abandoned and he embarked instead on studies of ethnology that would change the way Americans thought about their predecessors on the continent.

He was appointed Indian agent at the Soo in 1822, married the half Ojibwa daughter of the British agent there and immersed himself in tribal language and legends. Schoolcraft was well connected politically and in 1834 he received the patronage plum of agent at Mackinac.

The fur trade was coming to an end in this area and Schoolcraft saw that the Indian economy was being destroyed. He arranged for a system of payments to be made to tribal leaders over the course of ten years in return for the sale of 20 million acres of land. He earnestly hoped they would use the money to establish jobs and rebuild their economy. Instead, it only made the tribes dependent upon the government for their annual gifts.

A dormitory was built in 1838 to house the leaders during their stay on the island, and it remains standing as a museum of Indian life.

Schoolcraft continued his explorations and, eventually, he did succeed in finding the source of the Mississippi, at Lake Itasca, Minnesota. More important, he continued to work on his Indian studies. By 1839 he was recognized as the greatest authority on the subject in America. His "Algic Researches," published that year and filled with Ojibwa lore, caused a sensation in academic circles.

One very interested reader in Massachusetts was Henry Wadsworth Longfellow. Much of the material in his epic poem, "The Song of Hiawatha," was adapted from Schoolcraft's work. The success of the poem brought a romantic aura to the Native American past and influenced an entire school of historical fiction.

When Michigan was organized as a state, in 1836, Schoolcraft was asked to name several counties. He obliged with Indian-sounding names that used combinations of Ojibwa words but were invented by him. Many remain on the state map.

The Whigs came to power in Washington in 1841 and Schoolcraft lost his Mackinac post. He moved back East and continued to write about his findings on Indian culture, culminating in a six-volume history of American tribes published through the 1850s.

Schoolcraft died in 1864. But anyone who has been in Arenac, Iosco, Ogemaw or several other Michigan counties can still hear the names he left behind.

Fudge

The Island is known for its fudge and tourists are called "Fudgies"
photo courtesy John L. Russell

You will not be on Mackinac for more than, oh...maybe, five minutes before you realize that this candy is a very big deal here.

Fudge shops seem to occupy every other store on Main Street. The aroma wafts gently onto the street. Young candy-makers stand in the windows to roll out the confection on marble-top tables.

Fudge was not invented here. It was being sold in New England by the mid 19th Century. But it certainly has found a home on this island. In the minds of many visitors the words fudge and Mackinac are nearly synonymous.

Harry Murdick began selling it here in 1887 for the same reason it is sold today; so that the tourists will have a sweet souvenir to take home. Since fudge does not require refrigeration, it is the almost perfect vacation carry-out.

Murdick was the first to entice visitors by using large fans to send the candy smell outside the store. He also was a shrewd marketer. He made the rounds of county fairs throughout the Midwest, selling his distinctively labeled Mackinac variety.

Over 100 years of fudge

Success, as always, breeds imitation. Harold May, a pastry cook from Kansas, answered an ad by the Murdick family and soon opened his own place on Mackinac. He offered shipping service for those who didn't want to tote the stuff on the trip home. When their neighbors liked the taste, they could order some through the parcel post without ever going to Mackinac.

By the late 1940s, May and several Murdick siblings and relatives operated the biggest fudge shops. Then Harry Ryba arrived on the island. He had been making fudge at carnivals and fairs but soon realized that Mackinac was the mother lode. He opened his first store here in 1959 and began the practice of showing off the process in the front window.

Passers-by found the show irresistible, especially when Ryba, a born showman, urged his employees to put a little sass in the performance. The institution has spread throughout northern Michigan, and fudge is now a staple in most tourist areas.

There are, at least, half a dozen fudge shops on Main Street. The original, Murdick's, is still going strong, although Ryba usually wins media polls for best in the state.

And that is why tourists to Mackinac are called fudgies; albeit, rarely to their faces.

The Mighty Mac

The Mighty Mac opened in 1957

When you use that phrase up here, you are not referring to a new super-sized hamburger. This special sauce is all about a bridge.

The span that connects Michigan's Lower and Upper Peninsulas was opened on November 1, 1957, the culmination of 73 years of planning, dreaming and politicking.

When it was first proposed in the 1880s, the idea was waved off as wholly impractical. The completion of the Brooklyn Bridge had fired imaginations for more engineering achievements. Even railroad tycoon Cornelius Vanderbilt thought this bridge would be a fine thing. But in those years, the UP seemed as remote as the moon and the thought of such a span ever becoming profitable was considered unreasonable.

But it was an idea that wouldn't go away. When the automotive era dawned, it gathered momentum. Passage across the Straits was carried by a fleet of car ferries and at peak tourist seasons the wait could last for several hours. The lack of a convenient crossing was seen as a major inhibition to development of UP tourism; increasingly important as the copper and iron mines began shutting down.

In the 1920s, the newly-formed Michigan Highway Commission drew up a plan that called for a series of tunnels and causeways. By 1928, this had crystallized into a bridge. But the $30 million price tag was beyond the means of any government when the Depression arrived.

Finally, in 1950, a plan was introduced to build a bridge through revenue bonds that would be retired by user tolls. An accompanying feasibility study laid out hard figures on the boost to tourism this would accomplish on both sides of the span.

That was the clincher. A Bridge Authority issued $99.8 million in bonds, ground was broken in 1954 and three years later the Mighty Mac opened for business.

The bridge usually is listed as the third longest in the United States; behind New York's Verrazano-Narrows and San Francisco's Golden Gate. But that's only if you measure the length of the main span (3,800 feet at Mackinac). When you count the distance between anchorages, Mackinac checks in at 8,614 feet; much longer than the others. And when you include the approaches, Big Mac comes in at 5 miles, 44 feet. By that measure, only the Oakland-Bay Bridge is longer, but Mackinac goes the further uninterrupted distance over water.

It is a magnificent sight, one of Michigan's visual signatures. There are no turnouts on the bridge itself, but parks at both ends offer fine views of the Straits area.

A Labor Day walk across the bridge, led by the governor, is a state tradition. The bridge also has a good safety record, although it closes down under certain high-wind conditions. After a small car apparently was blown right off the span during a vicious winter storm, and with the recognition that high-profile SUVs are also susceptible to instability, the new safety procedures were put in place.

WHERE TO STAY

Grand Hotel. Cadotte Avenue. (906) 847-3331.

It isn't often that a hotel is also a prime tourist attraction. You'd better believe it. The crowds wanting to see the Grand's lobby and gardens grew so intense that it had to start imposing a charge to non-guests.

From the mainland, the sweeping, white veranda of the hotel is the most identifiable landmark on the island. From its hilltop perch, the Grand looms over the town like a rich dowager aunt.

It isn't for everyone. Those who want to leave coats and ties and dresses behind on a trip North, will not feel at home here. A dress code in all public areas is enforced after 6 p.m.

The magnificent Grand Hotel

While the hotel has been updated and amenities added, at its core it is still a Victorian facility. For some that is its greatest appeal. But the newer-is-better traveler will not be thrilled.

The Grand, in short, is a special experience, a journey in itself. It was built in 1887 as a promotion scheme, although it took two railroads and a steamship company to put the financing together. After a few missteps, its managers struck the tone that would appeal to the socially prominent families of the Midwest. These were people who were regarded, after all, as new money and not quite top drawer by the fashionable resorts of the East Coast, Newport and Bar Harbor. The Grand gave them a place of their own to preen.

Through the 1920s, it retained its position as the island's jewel. But when the Depression came, one of the first things to go, even among the wealthy, was an elaborate vacation. The Grand went bankrupt in 1931 after two dismal summers but was rescued by one its former employees, W. Stewart Woodfill.

He managed to guide it through the rough times, even though on some peak summer nights the number of guests could be counted on two hands and one toe. His nephew, Dan Musser, took over administration of the Grand in 1962. It had faded badly over the years and big spenders were taking their dollars elsewhere.

Musser began a major renovation that brightened up the lobby and restaurant, added some rooms and a second 9-hole golf course, refurbished the older accommodations. ("No two rooms are the same," it claims; and there are 381 of them.) He started promotions that extended its former 8-week season from May through October. Its heated outdoor pool, by the way, is named for Esther Williams, who filmed "This Time for Keeps" here in 1946.

The Grand once again lives up to its billing. Rates are high, starting at more than $400 a night for a double in peak season. But that includes a full breakfast and five-course dinner, and children under 11 are not charged. If you want to show up in March, you can get away with a nightly rate of less than one-third of the peak. But facilities are open on a limited basis.

There are several less expensive yet atmospheric alternatives on the island. They are also older properties and visitors should be prepared for a few missing amenities. But that's part of the island's ambience.

Island House. 1 Lake Shore Drive. (906) 847-3347.

It's the oldest hotel on the island, and a state historic site, just east of the center of town. Built in 1852, it originally stood on the harbor, but as it expanded it was moved back across the street. It is an imposing structure, with a front porch facing the water and two wings that nestle the core of the original building between them. The Island House has been entirely renovated, with 94 rooms and an indoor pool. Rates start at about $160 for a peak season double. There are bed and breakfast and dinner plans available, too.

The oldest hotel on Mackinac, the Island House

Lake View Hotel. 1 Huron Street. (906) 847-3384.

Just a few steps from the ferry docks, but across from the water, the Lake View is right in the middle of downtown activity. It features a great indoor pool in an atrium setting. It also claims to be the oldest hotel on Mackinac, although it was built 6 years after the Island House. How can that be? Because only the Lake View has been in continuous operation. There are 85 rooms, a full renovation was completed during the 1980s and it has added a spa and some whirlpool rooms. Rates are pegged just a bit higher than the Island House.

Chippewa Hotel. (906) 847-3341. Iroquois Hotel. (906) 847-3321.

The hotels are separately owned but there are lots of similarities between these two Main Street properties. Both sit right on the water and are named for Native American tribes. Both were built in 1902. The Chippewa is at the eastern end of Main, opposite Marquette Park; The Iroquois at the western end of the same street. The Iroquois has 40 rooms; the Chippewa 35.

These hotels were opened in response to Mackinac's great tourist boom of the early 1900s, when it first became the place to be seen. The Chippewa has answered many complaints by adding air conditioning units to its rooms that face the street. Normally, air is not needed on Mackinac, but the hotel is located at an especially busy location and street noise was a problem when the windows were open.

There is an outdoor pool at the Chippewa. The Iroquois has no pool but there is a small beach on the property. Both places have good restaurants on the premises, too. Expect to pay about $160-180 for rooms facing the street in the summer season; about $80-100 more than that for water views.

Mission Point Resort. (906) 847-3312. About one-third of a mile east of downtown.

Experiences can vary widely at this place, situated well away from the tourist bustle. It is a splendid location, with magnificent views down Lake Huron at the island's southeastern edge. But room upkeep can be slipshod and the food can be a source of unhappiness, too. At its best, though, it is a first-rate property.

Its history is certainly a bit different than most places on Mackinac. Most of Mission Point was built in 1954 as the campus of Moral Re-Armament. This religious-based organization grew up in America and England at the start of World War II. Its founder, Frank Buchman, called for a renewal of spiritual values, combined with a strong national military defense, as the best way to counter fascism and communism. For a while, it thrived here and even ran a film production studio.

But Buchman's death and a steady stream of negative publicity about right-wing ties sent MRA into decline in the 60s. For a while, it tried operating as a college based on MRA principles, but eventually was sold to evangelist Rex Humbard. Since the 1980s it has been run as a resort by a succession of ownerships.

There are 151 rooms in a main lodge and ancillary buildings. The pool is outdoors. Rates are competitive with in-town hotels. But be prepared for the comparatively remote location and the chance of uneven service.

Beds-and-Breakfast

Smaller inns abound on the island. These are four of the most historic and distinctive. Most B&Bs on the island open from May through October.

Bay View Inn. On the Marina, east of downtown. (906) 847-3295.

This yellow, waterside mansion was built for Chicago's Armour family of meat-packing fame in 1891. They never occupied it, though, selling it instead to the forebears of current innkeeper, Doug Yoder. There are 19 rooms. Town views go for $95 and up; a harbor view with a balcony starts at $155.

Haan's 1830 Inn. Huron Street, east of downtown. (906) 847-6244.

The name says it all. The date is when this 8-bedroom house was built and the Haans are the innkeepers. It is in a tranquil location, although you'll hear the bells once in a while from its next door neighbor, Ste. Anne's Catholic Church. You may even get a good view of one of the wedding processions that have become popular during the summer months. Rates go from $80-160.

Haan's is right next to Ste. Anne's

Metivier Inn. Market Street. (906) 847-6234.

The house was built in 1877 and its 21 rooms look out on one of the island's historic streets. One block up from Main Street, Market is an entirely different sort of scene. It is much less commercial, some buildings date from the late 18th Century and several others have been designated historic sites. A quiet setting, but just steps from the middle of everything. Rates run from $85-305.

The Inn at Stonecliffe. (906) 847-3355.

For those who really want to get away from the bustle, this is a good choice. It's well away from downtown, on a ridge in the northwestern part of Mackinac. One-third of its 48 rooms are in an early 19th Century home, Cudahy Manor. The rest are more contemporary accommodations in the Summer House. For obvious reasons, this is very popular with wedding parties, but be aware that it will be a trek to town for those who wish to mingle. There is an outdoor pool. Expect to pay a bit more than $100 for a garden-view room; significantly more if you want to look at the bridge.

Cottage Rentals

Under terms of their lease-holdings with the State of Michigan, most cottage owners must rent out their property for a minimum period each year. Although they are described as cottages, several are truly mansions, sleeping 10 or more people in ample comfort and room.

Many of them are late 19th Century gems, perched on bluffs above the harbor with incredible views of the water and Mackinac Bridge. They rent for $4,000-5,000 a week, and can be hard to reserve unless arrangements are made far in advance.

Sunset Condominiums (800) 473-6960 has a good assortment of classic homes and contemporary condos available. The Allen and Williams Cottages, just east of town and an easy walk from most places, are exceptional residences. The prize, however, may be the Casa Verano, a magnificent 5,000 square foot palazzo on the west bluffs, looking towards the bridge.

Mainland Choices

Hamilton Inn Select. Beachfront. Mackinaw City (231) 436-5493. 701 S. Huron St. (U.S. 23).

Right on the water with a long sand beach. Indoor pool. Ninety-six good-sized rooms. Free breakfast. Newer construction. A short walk to the Mackinac ferry dock and the downtown area. The best bet in this busy tourist town. Water view rooms will cost around $100 a night.

Best Western Harbour Pointe. St. Ignace. (906) 643-6000.
797 N. State St.

Another waterfront choice on Lake Huron, with good
views of Mackinac Island. St. Ignace is a bit quieter than
Mackinaw City with less of a tourist concentration. So this
side of the bridge is more of a true Northern experience.
Short walks to the ferry docks and downtown attractions.
Both indoor and outdoor pools. The BW chain took the
property over in 2004. Rates will average around $120 a
night in season for its 150 rooms.

Mainland Beds and Breakfast

Deer Head Inn. Mackinaw City. (231) 436-3337.
109 Henry Street.

If the sight of animal heads on the walls bothers you, this
will not be your kind of place. Nancy and Barry Dean have
turned this early 20th Century arts and crafts house into a
hunting camp sort of experience, with bear pelts and trophy
heads in all 5 rooms. The Hemingway Room, with a stone
fireplace, is the most elaborate and rents for $195 a night in
season. Other rooms go for $125-150. Henry Street is two
blocks in from the lake, running north from Central Avenue.

Brigadoon. Mackinaw City. (231) 436-8882. 207 Langlade St.

A contemporary structure--built in 1998--it, nonetheless,
manages to capture the ambience of the late Victorian era in
the Straits area. There are 8 rooms here, all of them with a
Northern theme, and innkeeper Sherree Hyde whips up some
great breakfast pastries. It's on a residential street, just a short
stroll to the ferry docks and downtown.

Camping

No overnight camping is allowed on Mackinac Island.
There are, however, a few choices in St. Ignace and
Mackinaw City.

Straits State Park, St. Ignace, has 275 campsites, some of them looking across the water and to the Mackinac Bridge. Established in 1924, the 334-acre park is just south of the U.S. 2 exit from the Mackinac Bridge. This is a popular and convenient facility. Indeed, some campers complain that the traffic noise from the bridge can be intrusive. Bathhouse facilities are available, May through October, but the campground is open all year. (906) 643-8620.

Lakeshore Park, St. Ignace, is a good choice for RVs, with 100 wider-than-usual sites. It is across the road from the water and has a lakeside picnic area as well as restroom facilities. Shuttles to the Mackinac ferries. Open May 1 to October 15. It is west on U.S. 2 from the Mackinac Bridge exit, then south on Pointe La Barbe Road. (906) 643-9522.

Foley Creek Campground is a unit of the Hiawatha National Forest, 6 miles north of St. Ignace and just off I-75, Exit 352, then south on the Mackinac Trail. There are 54 campsites here in a thickly wooded setting. The mile-long Horseshoe Bay hiking trail leads to a sandy beach on Lake Huron. (906) 786-4062.

Mackinaw Mill Creek Camping, Mackinaw City, has 600 sites, with 200 hook-ups, on the Lake Huron shore. A modern facility, a bit more than 2 miles south of town on U.S. 23. Shuttles to the ferries. Open Memorial Day to Labor Day. (231) 436-5584. In the off season, the phone is attended only on Saturdays, 9 a.m. to noon.

Wilderness State Park, Mackinaw City, has 250 campsites in a rustic setting (as the name would suggest). One of the units is on the lakeshore, another in the pine forest. The park is 11 miles west of Mackinaw City. There is a playground and first-rate hiking trails within its 8,000 acres on Lake Michigan. (800) 447-2757.

EATING OUT

The Grand's porch is 660 feet long

Grand Hotel. (906) 847-3331. Try the lunch buffet. You won't have to get all dressed up like you would at dinner and the Grand waives the fee to non-guests for the privilege of stepping inside its hallowed sanctum. The buffet goes on for almost as long as the famous front veranda. It will cost about $40 a person. But look at it this way. You will feel no need to order dinner that night and you get to enjoy a meal in one of the most splendid settings in the State.

The Jockey Club

The Jockey Club. (906) 847-3331. This is another of the Grand's restaurants, situated on the first tee of the hotel golf course. Less formal but an attractive dinner menu.

French Outpost. (906) 847-3772. It's on Cadotte Street, at the foot of the hill that leads up to the Grand. Right across the street from the Old Stone Church, with fine views of the hotel gardens. Casual setting but a nicely rounded steak-and-seafood menu and a good wine list.

Yankee Rebel. (906) 847-6349. The unusual name is a tribute to Ambrose Davenport, an American fur trader who refused to take an oath of allegiance to Britain when its forces captured Mackinac in 1812. He was paroled to Detroit for his pains while his family was held here. When he was allowed to return, in 1815, he took up farming and lived out his years on the island. The restaurant is known for its pot roast and salmon. It's on Astor Street, between Main and Market.

Horn's Gaslight Bar. (906) 847-6154. It's been a bar since Prohibition was repealed in 1933, but the place was run by the Horn family as a restaurant for a decade before that. It's an evening hot spot (or what passes for a hot spot on Mackinac) with a lively dance floor. The food is Southwestern style. On Main Street, in the heart of downtown.

Village Inn. (906) 847-3542. Serving up planked whitefish and homemade desserts since 1959, it's a reliable island standby. Located on Hoban Street, near the Arnold Ferry pier.

Carriage House at the Iroquois. (906) 847-3321. Meals with a waterfront view, either indoors or on the veranda. Good local fish entrees and a nice filet are its specialties. In the hotel on Main Street.

Casual Choices

Martha's Sweet Shop. If you don't think you can take another taste of fudge, this place cooks up the best cinnamon rolls on the island. Right on Main St., next to the taxi stand.

Inside the Fudge Shop

Tea Room at Fort Mackinac. A very nice luncheon experience on the hillside terrace of the fort, with spectacular views of the town and the Straits. The Grand Hotel caters and the emphasis is on light sandwiches and salads. One hitch: You have to pay the entrance fee to the fort.

The Pub and Oyster Bar. Just what the name says, pub-style eats and a raw bar. A filling burger, too. On Main Street, at the carriage stand.

Café Monet. The nicest coffee house on the island, off the lobby of the Murray Hotel, just across from the Arnold Ferry dock, on Main St. Excellent pastries.

Cannonball Drive-in. If you're biking around the island, this refreshment stand is a life-saver. Pop, hot dogs, burgers---that kind of fare. It's about halfway around the circuit at British Landing, the place where those sneaky Brits came ashore to capture the island in 1812.

Mary's Bistro. A casual, French-style café, with a patio that overlooks the harbor. Right near the Starline dock. This used to be the Dockside Inn and Mary has taken it a bit upscale.

Waterfront Patio Café. You order at the window and then take the food to the tables, many of which have harbor views. A good choice for families with restless younger members. On Hoban Street, near the Arnold pier.

Mackinaw City

Audie's Chippewa Room. (231) 436-5744. Best in town for its wide assortment of whitefish dishes prepared by a classically trained chef. An unpromising location, on the I-75 service drive, and the Native American motif is a bit worn. But the dinners are outstanding. At 314 N. Nicolet.

'Neath the Birches. (231) 436-5401. South on the Old Mackinaw Highway (Michigan 108). In an attractive wooded area, where forest creatures sometimes creep up to the windows and peer inside. Prime rib is good here.

Goldie's Cafe. A short drive on U.S. 31, to the village of Carp Lake, takes you to this terrific little waterfront restaurant. The breakfasts are wonderful and if you don't mind piling on the carbs ask for the raspberry pie. It's the family's traditional recipe. Goldie passed away in 1964, but her pies linger on.

St. Ignace

Dockside. (906) 643-7911. At 1101 N. State, near the downtown ferry docks. Views of the lake, very nice whitefish selections. Next to the Kewadin Casino Lakefront Inn. (The casino itself is a few miles away, on old U.S. 2.)

Driftwood. In downtown St. Ignace, this is a sports bar very popular with local residents, serving up the usual treats that sports bars do. It is also kind of a hangout for scuba divers from Straits Diving, down the block.

Taste of the Upper Peninsula. West from the Mackinac Bridge exit on U.S. 2. A place to sample the UP's food speciality, the pastie. Brought over from England by Cornish miners, the stuffed pie has become a regional staple. This place serves them up with the traditional beef filling, or with either turkey or vegetables.

Clyde's. West on U.S. 2. It boasts that this burger is the best in the UP. The locals love it.

ARRIVING ON MACKINAC

Kids love the ferry ride to the Island

Most people will reach the island aboard one of the three ferry lines from the mainland---**Arnold, Shepler's** or **Star.** All depart from both Mackinaw City, an 8-mile trip, or from St. Ignace, 5 miles away. Their docks are within a few blocks of each other both on the island and the mainland, and the crossing takes between 20 and 30 minutes.

Schedules are available for Arnold at (800) 542-8528; Shepler's at (800) 828-6157; and Star at (800) 638-9892. Most of them leave Mackinaw City at half hour intervals during the summer season. Parking is free at the docks.

The ferries usually suspend operations at the end of October and resume when the ice clears in April, although the Arnold Line continues from St. Ignace as long as ice conditions permit.

Bicycles can be taken aboard, but you must obtain a license on the boat to use them on the island. Otherwise, you can be ticketed. Unless you are a serious cyclist, the better idea is to rent one on the island (they are in plentiful supply) or through your hotel.

Hotel baggage wagons meet every arriving boat. If you are staying on the island, your luggage will have been tagged at the mainland dock and loaded for you upon arrival. But it's up to you to make sure that everything gets placed on the right cart. (Listen and learn: On the return trip, it's a good idea to leave a nice tip for the driver and baggage handler. Otherwise, you may be on the Mackinaw City ferry while your baggage winds up in St. Ignace.)

This is, by the way, one of the safest boat trips in the world. There have been no fatalities since service began in 1878.

WALKING AROUND MACKINAC

No matter what ferry line you came in on, at the end of the dock turn right. You will be on Main Street, in the midst of a Victorian confection.

Horses clop by, pulling freight wagons and passengers. Solo cyclists and tandem bikes stream past. Everyone else goes about their business on foot.

It won't take long before you learn to step delicately when you cross the street to avoid what horses drop. And your automotive-attuned eyes will quickly grasp the fact that getting run down by a bicycle is no bargain, either.

Walk gently, taking it all in. It takes a while to become acclimated, to slow down the pace of life.

To some people, such as the woman quoted at the start of this book, it's all phony, a fine kettle of kitsch. To most, however, a few hours or days spent away from the trappings of the 21st Century come as a welcome relief.

Main Street is just a few blocks long, and at its end, across from the water, is one of Mackinac's gathering places, **Marquette Park**. The green space is located right below the escarpment of **Fort Mackinac**. The space, in fact, once was used as the fort's stables.

On sunny days, the park is usually packed; filled with picnicking families, snoozing backpackers, summer campers on an outing letting off steam. The statue of **Father Jacques Marquette** (see Local Color) occupies its center.

Right across the street is the **State Park Visitor Center**. Take a few minutes to view the exhibits, get oriented and, if you plan to visit the historic sites, buy a ticket that includes the fort and five of these buildings. It will cost around $10 for adults. Most buildings open from early May to mid-October, but hours vary according to the season.

The Visitor Center is also a most convenient stop for restrooms.

The first stop should be the **Indian Dormitory**, in the northeastern corner of the park. As of this writing, it can only be viewed from the outside as it undergoes restoration. It was built in 1838 to lodge Native American leaders when they came to Mackinac to collect annual government payments. It is a handsome two-story structure with a center entrance and two sets of windows on either side. The style is late Federalist, the island's best example of that architectural mode.

The Indian visits ended in 1846 and for two decades the place stood empty. But in 1867 it became Mackinac's schoolhouse, and served that function for the next 97 years.

The **Bark Chapel** is also located in the park. This is a reconstruction of the earliest missionary church on the

The Bark Chapel

island, built in 1669 by Fr. Claude Dublon. This was the original location of the St. Ignace Mission, but it was too hard to reach in the winter months and closed after two years. Marquette then established the more sustainable mission on the Straits, at present day St. Ignace, in 1671.

The chapel has displays on the work of the French Jesuits among the Indians in this area. Admission is free.

Now continue walking east, along Huron Street, away from downtown. You will pass the **Island House,** built in 1852 and the oldest hotel on the island (described in the Where to Stay section.) The style is sort of a geographic anomaly, described as a mix of Victorian and Plantation.

The harbor is now on your right, and it is usually filled with some pretty impressive pleasure craft. Mackinac is the destination for the two most popular sailing races on the Great Lakes; one up Lake Michigan from Chicago and the other up Lake Huron from Port Huron. The harbor is an especially lively spot at those times.

You will pass a row of private homes, some B&Bs, and soon the steeple of **Ste. Anne's** will come into view. This soaring Victorian church is the lineal descendant of the little bark chapel in Marquette Park. The Jesuit mission was moved to St. Ignace, then crossed the Straits to Mackinaw City in 1742. When the British garrison moved to Mackinac in 1780 the church came with it, transported back to its original home.

It was first placed near the current Arnold Line dock downtown. But as that area grew too congested, Ste. Anne's was moved here in the late 1820s. The old church was replaced by the present structure 50 years later. The interior is open whenever services are not being held. Besides some old pews and stained glass windows, the church is noted for the fresco of Ste. Anne, depicted in a Mackinac setting, behind the high altar. It is believed to have been a part of the original church building.

There is a small museum in the basement with displays on the church's long history.

Mackinac's historic churches have become popular sites for summer weddings and must be reserved many months ahead of time for these happy events. No short engagements can make it here.

The most requested is the **Mission Church,** two blocks further along this road. This is the oldest church building in

Little Stone Congregational Church

Michigan, dating from 1830, and it also is regarded as the best example of colonial New England church architecture in the Great Lakes area.

It was originally a Presbyterian mission, opened by Rev. William Ferry. He had come to the island to educate Indian youths and prepare them for useful trades. Many of them actually worked on its construction. It became the parish church of Fort Mackinac, and officials of the American Fur Co. regularly attended Sunday services.

But as the fur trade died out and the ferrys left the island, the congregation dwindled. It closed only 8 years after its completion, was used briefly by parishioners of Ste. Anne's when their new church was being built and finally was taken over by the State in the 1890s.

It has been run as an historic site since then and restored to its 1830s appearance. The Mission Church is affiliated with no denomination and has no resident clergy, but throughout the summer, weddings go on here almost daily. Since there are no changing facilities inside, bridal parties arrive in carriages, fully dressed for the ceremony. It has become one of the island's most cheerful sights and tourists with cameras are almost as numerous as the invited guests.

Admission to the church is included in the State Park package plan. It is open daily, noon to 4 p.m., mid-June to mid-August. Weddings must be timed around these hours.

Continue along the road to **Mission Point.** The resort here, on the former campus of the Moral Re-Armament organization, is described in the Where to Stay section. In the broad expanse of lawn that runs down to the lake, several Adirondack chairs are usually available. Plop yourself down in one and take a little while to absorb some of the loveliest scenery on the lakes. You can easily get lost in your own personal version of "Somewhere in Time."

Rising behind you is the **East Bluff,** with several expansive summer homes along its edge. In the Mission Point area, this 125-foot ridge is called **Robinson's Folly.** No one is quite sure why.

It probably refers to Capt. Daniel Robertson, who was

the commandant at Fort Mackinac in the late 1780s. The legends about him have several versions, most of them involving him and an Indian princess (or sometimes her father) leaping to their doom from this precipice. According to the official records, Robertson left Mackinac quick and well in 1787, but his alleged folly remains.

We don't want to puzzle over this too long because there is much more to see. Retrace your steps toward town. Just past Ste. Anne's take a right on the side street. Another right will bring you to the **Butterfly House,** one of the island's delightful little sideshows.

You enter an enclosed garden with around 800 butterflies, brought here from around the world, flying around freely. Children are fascinated by their beauty and by the exhibits that show how they emerge from the pupa. It really has no intrinsic relationship to Mackinac but it's a wonderful stop anyhow.

Admission is $5 for adults, and it is open from early May to mid-October, 10 a.m. to 6 p.m.

Continue on to **Marquette Park,** and at its far end turn right on Fort Street. At the southern corner of Market is the **McGulpin House,** which may be the oldest building on the island. It probably was built in Mackinaw City and was brought to Mackinac with the British garrison in 1780.

The house was originally located behind Ste. Anne's. (That street, on which the Butterfly House is located, is still called McGulpin.) He didn't build it, though. The architecture is French-Canadian, with a steeply pitched roof and distinctive placement of connecting logs. This was probably built as the home of a fur trader and then was purchased in 1817 by the fort baker, William McGulpin. The house was moved here in recent years.

It is open daily, 11 a.m. to 6 p.m., in summer and included in the State Park admission ticket.

Right across Market Street is the **American Fur Company** store, now a memorial to the medical work of Dr. William Beaumont (see Local Color). This is where his patient, Alexis St. Martin, was wounded in 1822 in the accidental shooting that led to Beaumont's landmark studies of the human digestive system.

The building was restored in 1954 by the Michigan Medical Society and turned into a museum honoring the physician. Some of his instruments are displayed here, and there are also exhibits on how his experiments with St. Martin were conducted. It is also open daily, 11 a.m. to 6 p.m. as part of the State Park ticket.

Those who do not choose to walk up to the fort, or are physically unable to make the climb, should skip ahead a few paragraphs to where the walk down Market Street continues. Otherwise, keep walking up Fort Street.

The **Gothic Revival Trinity Episcopal Church,** built in 1882, was closely involved with life at the fort. Chancel chairs were carved by soldiers who regularly attended services here and the walnut altar also was crafted by local woodworkers. It is still an active congregation.

A great view through the gate

Continue up the incline to the entry gate of **Fort Mackinac.** Its first commandant, Major Patrick Sinclair, engineered the fortifications and did quite a job. They have stood up, with some restoration, since 1780. Sinclair, fearful of an overland attack during the Revolutionary War, ordered the entire British garrison of Fort Michilimackinac, at Mackinaw City, transferred to the island. A payment of

5,000 pounds to local tribes nailed down the land purchase. As we have seen earlier in this chapter, entire buildings were transported across the ice from the mainland to Mackinac. Sinclair's goal was to defend the harbor and repel any chance of an American naval landing. This is where the heavy guns were concentrated behind walls three feet thick.

(When the British were faced with the task of retaking Mackinac during the War of 1812, they avoided Sinclair's defenses simply by landing on the opposite side of the island and taking it by a ground attack from the rear.)

The penny pinchers in London were outraged at Sinclair's expenditures. He was recalled in 1782 and never returned to Mackinac.

But the fort he built remained an active military post for the next 113 years. The Officers' Stone Quarters is the oldest building on the grounds, surviving almost intact from the day the fort opened. The south sally port, which is now the main entrance, also dates from the original structure. The Governor's Summer Residence, built by a local merchant in 1902 and taken over by the State in 1945 as a vacation home for Michigan's chief executive, is on the grounds, too. It's open for tours on Wednesdays, 9:30 to 11:30 a.m., early June to late August.

In most cases, buildings have been restored to their appearance of the 1820s and 30s under the American military. Costumed guides, re-enacting the roles of soldiers and fort artisans of that period, are stationed at the major structures. There are also demonstrations of military drills, musketry and cannon bursts throughout the day.

The fort is open daily, 9:30 a.m. to 6 p.m., from mid-June to late August. Hours can vary at other times of year, from May through mid-October. The fort is part of the State Park admissions package. If you are here in the evening, stay for the flag-folding ceremony conducted by the Boy Scouts. It is quite moving.

Descend the ramp from the fort and retrace your steps back to Market Street. This is Mackinac's most historic thoroughfare, with many buildings associated with the

American Fur Co. along its length.

Some of the residences built during its heyday remain in private hands and a few now are B&Bs. This is also where the town's administrative offices are located.

You will pass the fur company warehouse and the adjoining home of its chief agent, Robert Stuart (see Local Color). This was the business and social hub of the island from 1817 until John Jacob Astor sold his company in 1834. Stuart and his wife, Elizabeth, entertained visitors and housed company officials when they visited.

The house became the first hotel on the island in the 1840s. Later in the century, it combined with the warehouse to create the Astor House, the first large-scale inn on Mackinac. President U.S. Grant stayed there on his visit to the island in the 1870s. A porch connected the two structures but it was torn down shortly after the hotel closed in the 1920s.

The two buildings, which underwent restoration in the late 1990s, are run as a museum of the fur trade by the town of Mackinac. Some original items belonging to the Stuarts and fort commandant Sinclair are displayed. Hours are the same as the other island museums, although it not part of the State Park admissions ticket.

You'll pass city hall, built in 1834, one of the oldest in the State. It also served as the Mackinac County courthouse until the county seat was moved to St. Ignace, for the usual reason of accessibility, in 1882.

In a few more steps you'll come to the **Biddle House,** built by a fur trader who was related to the famed Philadelphia family. There is some dispute over whether this house or the McGulpin House, which we passed a little while ago, is the oldest on the island. Since the McGulpin residence was moved here from the mainland, the Biddle House is, indisputably, the oldest home actually built on Mackinac.

Edward Biddle was an independent fur trader in the years before Astor consolidated control of the business. His comfortable home was probably built during the first year of British occupation, in 1780. It is now a museum of domestic life on the island, with ongoing demonstrations of 18th Century crafts.

In the rear of the house is the **Benjamin Blacksmith Shop,** dating from the 1870s and originally located near the foot of the Grand Hotel. The opening of the hotel, in 1887, brought large scale tourism to the island and Robert Benjamin prospered. He later served as the island's postmaster and mayor and the county sheriff.

The shop was run as a family enterprise for its entire existence, closing in 1967. It was rebuilt at this location from the original materials, and displays much of the equipment the Benjamins actually used. It is now run as a museum, and with the Biddle House is part of the State Park admissions package.

Market Street ends at Cadotte Street, where the Grand Hotel property begins. Turn right to take the short walk to its entrance. You will pass the **Little Stone Church,** built in 1900, another of Mackinac's popular wedding venues. Many of the island's socially prominent families attended services here and some of its glass was created in the Tiffany workshops. It remains an active house of worship.

The entrance to the Grand is on the left, with its gardens stretching down the hill. When the hotel began imposing an entrance fee for non-guests in the 1980s, it caused a stir of protest. But the Grand was concerned about tourists overwhelming the paying customers. Ten bucks a head may sound a bit pricey, but this is one of the country's great hotel landmarks and well worth a look.

As mentioned in the Places to Eat section, you can avoid the fee by reserving a spot at the luncheon buffet. If you timed this walk properly, the food should be ready right about now.

The Bicycle Circuit

Ther are no cars on Mackinac Island

There is no better way of getting to know Mackinac than to take the 8-mile bicycle ride around its perimeter road: Michigan 185. It's the only State highway that does not carry automotive traffic, although you will have to stay alert for aggressive cyclists who can't seem to leave their bad driving habits on the mainland.

If you are physically able to make the circuit, do it. You can see the island at your own pace, and not on other people's schedules; stopping where you like to take pictures of the bridge or the Round Island Lighthouse, gathering stones, having a snack. The ride is absolutely level. There are no uphill climbs, unless you choose to explore the middle of the island.

There is no problem getting a bike. Main Street is loaded with rental companies. Most rates start at $4 an hour, with reductions for full day and half day rentals. There will also be a security deposit required.

The Mackinac Island Bicycle Shop (906) 847-6337, on Main Street, is the place to go for information on more challenging rides to the island interior. It is also a point of departure for group tours; at 10 a.m., Monday through Saturday, in season, and also at 7 p.m. on Friday and

Saturday. These are designed for experienced, fit riders. Call for rates and more information.

Most cyclists choose to make the perimeter trip in a counter-clockwise rotation. You will first pass the landmarks described in the walk to Mission Point in the previous section.

After that, look for the turnout to Dwightwood Spring, a small memorial established in 1905 by a family who owned a nearby cottage to honor their late son. The spring, one of many on the island, still gushes, but the water is not recommended for consumption.

A little beyond this is the stairway to **Arch Rock.** If you don't feel like making the 150-foot climb, you can look up and see the dramatic 50-foot wide limestone formation that spans two cliffs. The view from the top is wonderful. But if you want to save your energy for the bicycle, be content with the view from the ground and peddle on.

Arch Rock is 150 feet above Lake Huron

You will soon reach the **Wildflower Trail,** a 300-yard footpath that is well worth following. Signs along the way explain the habitats through which you are walking and identify the flowers on the path.

Once past **Pointe Aux Pins,** the northern extremity of the island, you will see great views of the Upper Peninsula and the Mackinac Bridge.

British Landing marks the halfway point of the trip and it is an excellent place for a refreshment stop at the little food stand.

You'll complete the circuit, with a stop at **Devil's Kitchen,** a limestone cavern that was carved by lake waters when they reached much higher levels than they do now.

You will now be running alongside the splendid homes on West Bluff. Finally, the **Boardwalk,** which extends along the water for about half a mile from the Grand Hotel grounds, will mark the way back to the middle of town.

The mainland also offers worthwhile biking experiences because of **Michigan's Rails to Trails program.** An extensive network of tracks was built in this area during the lumbering boom. But the trains haven't run for years and their grades have been converted into hiking-biking trails.

From Mackinaw City, the path heads south, paralleling U.S. 23 along the Lake Huron shore. The highway is almost always in earshot, if not in sight, but the ride is scenic.

A more authentic Northern experience is the **St. Ignace Trail.** It leaves from the center of town and runs right into the heart of **Hiawatha National Forest.** In most places, there are no roads at all. The trail runs across the width of the UP, so you can ride until you're whacked and then turn around.

There are 16 miles of hiking and biking trails in **Wilderness State Park.** This is one of the finest getaways in the Lower Peninsula for those who like to lose the modern world. It is so good for that, in fact, that park officials strongly recommend that everyone heading into the forests there carry a compass and a map.

Horse and Carriage Tours

The easiest and most historically correct way to see the island is to be pulled around by a horse. This is how the first tourists explored Mackinac. In 1869, of course, when the first carriage license was issued, this was an unexceptional mode of transportation on or off the island. The automobile was still three decades in the future.

An elegant way to travel the Island

Now it is part of Mackinac's special charm, riding in a conveyance that is rarely seen outside of Amish communities on the mainland.

Mackinac Island Carriage Tours claims to be the world's oldest continuously operating livery. It may also be the largest, with a stable of 400 horses and 100 carriages. The company also provides cab service (see below) and contracts for the island's street sweeping service and funeral processions. In the winter, it offers sleigh rides.

Its standard island tours, which last an hour and 45 minutes, leave from the Main Street carriage stand. It's hard to miss, with all those horses standing there. Call (906) 847-3307 for information on exact schedules and rates, but expect to pay around $16 for adults, $7.50 for children under 12. The tours generally run from 9 a.m. to 5 p.m. during the summer; until 3 p.m. from mid-May to mid-June, and after Labor Day through October.

Private group tours can be arranged through their main office.

The carriage rides take visitors into the island's hilly interior, a more strenuous excursion than the walk and bike ride outlined earlier. Geological formations, scenic viewpoints and historic points of interest are included. Most of them are described in the Other Things to See section.

An added stop on all the tours is **Surrey Hills,** the company stables, with a collection of antique Mackinac carriages and surreys and some working Clydesdales.

If you are feeling ambitious, you can rent your own horse and buggy at **Jack's Livery** (906) 847-3391. Expect to pay $45 an hour for two people; $55 an hour for four. It's on Mahoney Avenue, which runs off Cadotte Avenue, near the Grand Hotel. You are not allowed to take the buggies into the middle of town, though.

There are riding horses available for rent there and a good system of marked trails to lead you through the island's interior.

You can also arrange a hayride at **Mackinac Island Service Company,** at (906) 847-3713.

Taxis

No use trying to whistle or wave for a cab here. That won't work. You either have to call in advance, at (906) 847-3323, or go to the taxi stand, on Main at Astor streets. The cabs operate as jitneys and will also pick up other passengers with reservations en route. So give yourself plenty of time to get where you're going.

WEDDINGS

As mentioned previously, a wedding in one of Mackinac's historic churches has become an adventure in romance.

Many couples choose to make their own arrangements by directly contacting clergy in the area. But for those who eschew long-distance affairs there is one resident wedding consultant. Carol Ebel runs **For the Love of Mackinac** (888) 847-3691 and she specializes in making the special day go as smoothly as a skipping stone.

BOAT TRIPS

To see Mackinac at a more leisurely pace than the ferries allow, there are catamaran tours aboard the *Mackinaw Breeze*. It sails from the dock behind the Chippewa Hotel.

There are four scheduled sailings every day during the summer; at noon and at 2, 4 and 6 p.m. Trips last approximately 90 minutes and make a full circuit of the harbor area; past the Round Island Lighthouse and near neighboring Bois Blanc Island (which made news back in the 80s when its one-room schoolhouse had a total of one student).

Reservations should be made in advance, although walk-ons are welcome if the 26-passenger boat is not filled. Call (906) 847-8669. Fares are $30 a person. The tour most in demand is the 6 p.m. sailing with views of late summer sunsets. The *Breeze* can also be chartered for half and full day trips.

(If you can't make the sunset cruise, a good alternative is to simply walk west from town on the Boardwalk. Picnic tables are set out along the shore for those who want to share a carry-out meal in this romantic setting.)

For a charter fishing trip, try the *Dream Seaker*. The 27-foot long vessel can accommodate six guests. Its home port is Pickford, in the Upper Peninsula, but it will pick up passengers in the Mackinac area.

Its captain, James Shutt, has extensive experience in these waters, which give up fine lake trout and walleye. Remember, for a brief time between the end of the fur trade and the start of the tourism industry, fishing was the economic backbone of the Straits area.

Reservations can be made at (888) 634-3419. Rates start at $320 for a half day trip. The season runs from May 15 to October 15.

Tip: If you're thinking of doing some fishing, you could do worse than to hang out at the **Pink Pony Lounge,** at the **Chippewa Hotel.** This is an established hangout for boaters and fishermen, and if you're properly affable you may be able to find out where the best locations are.

The ferry boat lines also run special tours. One of the best is **Shepler's** cruise to four lighthouses around the Straits area, some of them situated in magnificent scenic locations and inaccessible by any other public transportation. The three lines also offer sunset cruises into Lake Michigan. For schedules and rates call the lines. Shepler's (800) 828-6157; Arnold (800) 542-8528; Star (800) 638-9892.

DIVING

The **Straits of Mackinac Bottomland Preserve** is an unforgettable diving experience, with nine major wrecks to explore within its 148 square miles.

This can still be a treacherous area in bad weather for the huge lake freighters, as they maneuver through the 5-mile wide gap between the two peninsulas. As recently as 1965, the *Cedarville,* a 558 foot long steel-hulled vessel, went down after colliding with another ship in fog. The oldest wreck in the area is the *Sandusky,* a twin-masted schooner which sank in a nasty autumn storm in 1856 with its cargo of grain.

Best place for maps and equipment is **Straits Diving,** at 587 N. State Street, St. Ignace. It operates the 42-foot long *Rec Diver* on daily trips to the best diving spots. Reservations should be made well in advance at (866) 329-3483.

OTHER THINGS TO SEE

East and West Bluffs. Some of the most decorative summer homes on Mackinac are situated along these ridges above the water. They are primarily in Victorian and Queen Anne styles, with turrets and widow's walks and all sorts of gee-gaws wonderful to view.

These two bluff areas lie on either side of downtown but are not directly connected. They can be explored on foot or by bicycle, if you are able to handle the climb.

Garrison Road Area. This road runs from Fort Mackinac into the interior heights of the island and leads to some of its most scenic attractions.

At the corner of Rifle Range Road is **Skull Cave.** The limestone opening was formed when these heights were at the water's edge of an island, 11,000 years ago. Its historic importance is that the cave is believed to be the one that British trader Alexander Henry described as his refuge during Pontiac's Rebellion. Only a handful of Brits escaped the massacre at Fort Michilimackinac, on the mainland, in 1763.

Henry, who had become friendly with several Indian leaders, was spirited off to the island and concealed here. He was told that his pursuers would not enter because it was filled with skulls, whether human or animal Henry couldn't tell. Whichever, he survived to tell the tale.

There is a footpath that leads from this area to Fort Holmes, the highest point on the island, 325 feet above Lake Huron. The British seized this vantage point during their invasion in 1812 and brought in heavy guns to force the surrender of Fort Mackinac, right below.

Little remains of the fort but some grassy outlines and the ruins of its walls. It is an evocative place, though, a world removed from the tourist tumult.

The path also leads to **Point Lookout.** The view from this place not only includes the lake far below but also **Sugar Loaf.** This is a cone-shaped limestone formation that once formed part of a cliff that was worn away by erosion. As with Skull Cave, it once stood on the shore of prehistoric **Lake Algonquin.** This was a holy site among Native Americans, who believed its isolated majesty was the abode of the Great Spirit.

There are also caves and natural phenomena on other parts of the island, including Cave in the Woods and Crack in the Woods. A map of walking trails is advisable if you wish to explore them. That can be obtained at the Mackinac State Park visitors' center opposite Marquette Park.

One of the most unforgettable parts of a walk into the island's interior is the wildflowers. They are protected by law and bloom with stunning diversity throughout Mackinac's forests. You will find trillium, lady slippers, violets and a host of others in the spring; buttercups and wood lilies in summer. The wetlands have orchids and fringed gentian. There are fields of color almost anywhere you look at any season.

It is unusual to find any large mammals on the island. The occasional deer or even a wolf will turn up after crossing the ice in winter. But that is a rarity. There are, however, plenty of bats.

There is an abundance of birdlife, though, because Mackinac lies on a well-traversed migration route. You can see eagles in spring, snowy owls in winter, warblers and buntings in summer. A guide to the island's plants and birds can be purchased at the Visitor Center, opposite Marquette Park.

MACKINAW CITY ATTRACTIONS

Colonial Michilimackinac. Pontiac is one of the great figures of Native American history. A born political leader, he was able to persuade the tribes of the Great Lakes area to put aside their differences and unite in 1763 to drive out the British.

He had no problems with the French. They came to trade and bring Christianity. Aside from a few settlements they did not appear to have permanent designs on the land. But the British were different, and that made them a danger. After the French lost their war with England, Pontiac decided the time was right to strike against this threat.

He came close to realizing his goal, capturing almost every outpost west of Niagara Falls and laying siege, unsuccessfully, to Detroit. But it was at Mackinaw City that his rebellion saw its greatest and bloodiest achievement.

On a sparkling June day, a group of Indians approached

the fort to play a game of lacrosse. The tiny British force of 20 men, enthused about such a welcome diversion from dull garrison life, came outside to watch.

Indian women ringed the players. No one thought it odd that they wore blankets on such a warm afternoon.

At the prearranged signal, the women threw aside their blankets and the men took up the weapons that were hidden underneath. They then set about to slaughter every soldier and British trader they could find.

A few civilians escaped, hidden by horrified French residents of the fort and rescued later by friendly Indians.

This was the high water mark for Pontiac. Detroit could not be taken, and three months later, when supplies and reinforcements arrived, the Indian alliance broke apart. Michilimackinac was reoccupied and manned by the British until removal of the garrison to Mackinac in 1780.

This fort was abandoned and slowly returned to nature. But in 1959, almost two centuries after its most terrible event, restoration work began on Michilimackinac.

The work had to be much more extensive than at Fort Mackinac, which had come through its couple hundred years in fairly decent shape. Today, however, Michilimackinac is an excellent military restoration. Its major structures---barracks, residences, store, church---have been returned to their original appearance, or as closely as archeological and historical research allowed. It also conducts archeological field trips for visitors. Call the number below for availability.

Guides play the roles of actual occupants of the fort. The high point of the year, however, is the re-enactment of the massacre, on Memorial Day weekend.

The fort is open daily from early May through October. Hours are 9 a.m. to 6 p.m. in summer; earlier closing at other times. Admission is $9, although a combination ticket for other attractions (see below) is available for $18. (231) 436-4100.

Old Mill Creek. This sawmill began operations in 1790 and is regarded as the first industrial complex in the northern lakes area. It was run by the Campbell family for about 30 years after being granted the concession to cut and supply the lumber needed for construction on Mackinac Island. It shut down sometime around 1819.

The place was rediscovered in the early 1970s by an amateur archeologist, a schoolteacher in nearby Cheboygan. Replicas of the mill, a dam, a colonial-era workshop and other buildings stand near their original location on the site.
Costumed guides offer demonstrations of the work that was done here.

The park is located 3 miles south of Mackinaw City, on U.S. 23. Hours are the same as Colonial Michilimackinac, and it also is part of the Mackinac Historic Parks admission package. (231) 436-4100.

Thunder Falls Family Water Park. This is Mackinaw City's newest family attraction and it is a doozey. Twelve slides, the biggest wave pool in Michigan, 20 acres of entertainment. It opened in 2004. Rates for adults are in the $25 range, for kids under four-feet tall it's around $16. The park is located at 1028 S. Nicolet, south on the Mackinaw Highway.

Maritime Park. It stretches east along the Mackinaw City lakefront from the base of the Mackinac Bridge and offers postcard view of the Straits, the island and bridge. The restored Mackinac Point Lighthouse, dating from 1892 and reopening for visits in June, 2004, is the centerpiece of the park. The light operated until the bridge opened in 1957. It had only four tenders over its 65-year history.

The light is part of the Mackinac Historic Parks. A separate admission of $6 is charged to enter and climb to the top.

ST. IGNACE ATTRACTIONS

Marquette Mission Park and Museum of Ojibwa
Culture. This was the site of the 1671 mission established
by Fr. Jacques Marquette. Five years later, it became his
burial place.

The grave was lost after the mission was abandoned.
But after its rediscovery in 1877 the site proved to be one
of the richest archeological troves on the lakes. Hundreds
of artifacts of French and Native American culture have
been unearthed here, and the Huron village that lay outside
the mission has been reconstructed. There is a traditional
longhouse, and crops that might have been planted by the
Huron have been reintroduced to the site. A statue of the
priest marks the presumed site of his grave.

The Ojibwa are now the most populous Indian group in
the Upper Peninsula and a museum of their culture is located next door to the mission. Exhibits relate the history of
the people, their family structure, crafts and relationship to
the natural environment.

The park and museum are located downtown, at 500
North State Street. The museum is open daily, 10 a.m. to 8
p.m., July 1 to Labor Day; shorter hours, May and June.
Admission is $2. (906) 643-9161.

The Father Marquette National Memorial is part of
Straits State Park, just off the UP end of the Mackinac
Bridge. There are interpretive displays and some trails that
lead to stunning views of the Straits and the bridge.
Unfortunately, a museum was destroyed by fire in 2000 and
many irreplaceable historical artifacts were consumed.
Open all day, all year. $4 per vehicle. (906) 643-8620.

Huron Boardwalk. This lakeside promenade offers a
pleasant stroll across the street from the town's business
district. Along the way are exhibits relating to St. Ignace's
maritime history, including several artifacts from notable
shipwrecks on the Straits.

Castle Rock. One of the most venerable roadside tourist sites in the UP This glacial formation is 200 feet tall and 179 steps lead to the top for views of the surrounding countryside. There is a 50-cent charge to make the climb. It's 3 miles north of St. Ignace, just off I-75. Open May to late September, daily, 9 a.m. to dusk. (906) 643-8268.

SCENIC DRIVES

If you feel compelled to get in some drive time after visiting the island, there are several side trips worth making in the Straits area.

U.S. 23 between Mackinaw City and Cheboygan has Lake Huron on the east for the entire route. You'll have views of Bois Blanc Island and pass Mill Creek State Park on the way. In Cheboygan, there is a lakeside park with a beach, the restored Opera House and the Coast Guard ice cutter, *Mackinaw,* which welcomes visitors when it is in its berth on the Cheboygan River.

C-81 runs west from Mackinaw City along Lake Michigan and leads to Wilderness State Park, with its unusual geological formations, wildflowers and stunning views of the lake.

U.S. 2 goes west from St. Ignace into the Hiawatha National Forest along the northern shore of Lake Michigan. There are several places to pull over and explore its remote beaches. This road can get crowded during summer, though, because it is the only through highway in the area.

SHOPPING

Unless you're bonkers over fudge, this is not what you'd call a shopper's paradise. Heavy on knick-knacks in the main tourist areas, but much of the stuff is routine and overpriced. You'll find an assortment of clothing and crafts stores. But if you're avidly into shopping, you're in the wrong place.

A short list of shops of more than passing interest:

Nadia's Fashion Shop, with the largest selection of footwear and clothing on the island.

Mackinac Lapidary features custom jewelry with a Mackinac theme.

Mackinac Outfitter and Marine Supply is the place to go if the weather turns chilly and you brought only short sleeves.

Lilacs and Lace, crafts and art in the Carousel Shops, on Market Street.

Doud's Mercantile, which claims to be the oldest grocery store in Michigan, is also a good place to linger. It was established in 1854, and when the original store burned down in 1943 it moved to the present location, the corner of Main and Fort streets. Good for carry-out sandwiches and other essentials for a picnic.

Best bookstore on the island is the aptly-named **Island Bookstore.** It's on Main Street, and open from 10 to 10 daily. There is a branch in Mackinaw City, at 215 E. Central. Same hours, with a coffee shop, too.

The only mall in the area is **Mackinaw Crossings,** in the midst of downtown Mackinaw City. This is a pleasant enough, open-air setting with a few dozen shops, many of them featuring items of local interest. It also has the only movie complex in the area and a central court where live entertainment is scheduled in the summer months. The Crossings opens from May through October.

St. Ignace's shopping area runs along N. State Street. It is a rather utilitarian strip, however, since St. Ignace, unlike the other two Straits communities, is a place where people actually go about their lives 12 months of the year.

There are two galleries worth checking out on the street. **MahDezeWin,** at 330 N. State, features the work of Indian artist, James Simon Mishibinijima, who is Canadian. He works with bright colors and often employs birch as part of his work. **Mackinac Straits Photography,** at 208 N. State, displays the work of David Black, who specializes in the scenery and animal life of the area.

Totem Village is a venerable roadside attraction that specializes in Native American souvenirs and moccasins. It's at 1230 West U.S. 2.

GOLF

Open space is at a premium on Mackinac Island. So the golf options are limited to one 18-hole course, a 9-hole course and an 18-hole putting green.

The **Jewel** is the Grand Hotel's course. Actually, it is a combination of two 9-hole courses built 93 years apart.

The front nine is the **Grand,** opened in 1901 and redesigned by architect Jerry Matthews in 1987. It is fairly short (2,405 yards from the blue tees), but the greens are artfully positioned and the terrain hilly. It also has distractingly gorgeous views over the town.

Here's the good part. If you're playing the full 18 holes, you get into a carriage after the ninth green and travel about a mile and a half to the 10th tee. This second course is called the Woods, because it was cut through a hardwood forest. Matthews also designed it, in 1994. It is 600 yards longer than the Grand and the fairways dangerously narrow. The Woods also features a nice restaurant with catering by the hotel.

Expect to pay $100 for 18 holes if you're not staying at the Grand; $80 if you are. Tee times at (906) 817-3331.

Wawashkamo is the oldest course on the island, and is believed to be the oldest continuously played course in Michigan. It is designated as a state historic site. Built by a group of summer residents in 1898, it was laid out by Scottish golfer Alex Smith in the links style. A restoration one century later retained that plan, with natural grass in the fairways and some escape-proof thistle and heather in the roughs.

This is a unique 19th Century golfing experience and it offers an option to extend play to 18 holes by moving the tee placements and using antique balls and clubs. The course is located in the island's interior, on a War of 1812 battlefield, off British Landing Road. A taxi is the best bet for getting there.

The fee is $50 for 18 holes and $30 for a cart. Call (906) 847-3871.

The Greens at Mission Point claims to be an authentic golfing experience, only with all the tees and fairways removed. Each of the 18 greens is sculpted and trapped just as they would be on a championship course. There are even water hazards to contend with.

The course is on the lakefront, just outside the entrance to the resort. The fee is $12. Call (906) 847-3312.

The nearest 18-hole course on the mainland is the **Mackinaw Golf Club.** This is another Jerry Matthews design, opened in 1997, a nicely done bent grass surface in a pleasant north woods setting. It's long and straight at 3,202 yards. Call (231) 431-7590 for tee times and fees.

There is a 9-hole course, the **St. Ignace Golf and Country Club,** just west of town, at 915 W. U.S. 2. Fees range from $9 to $20. Tee times are necessary. (906) 643-8071.

BEACHES

Unless you are a paid-up member of the Polar Bear Club, swimming in these waters will have limited appeal. Dips in the Straits are recommended only for strong, experienced swimmers.

However, the pebbly beaches on the east side of Mackinac Island, on Lake Huron, are good for families who don't mind the cold. The bottom is shallow here, so wear some foot protection for those nasty stones. There are no lifeguards at any of the island's beaches.

The best beach in the entire area is at **Wilderness State Park,** west of Mackinaw City, on Lake Michigan's Big Stone Bay. It is sandy and the protected waters of the bay are marginally less frigid than the open lake. **Cecil Bay** is a bit closer to Mackinaw City along C-81. It is part of the Emmet County park system and has a good sandy beach.

The small **Kiwanis Beach** is on State St., near downtown St. Ignace. You can also pull over amid the dunes on U.S. 2, west of St. Ignace, where the beach stretches along for miles on the north shore of Lake Michigan. No lifeguards or facilities.

There are no public swimming pools on Mackinac Island, although several of the hotels have pools for their guests.

WINTER

For those who really, really love winter, Mackinac can be unforgettable. The hotels and almost all tourist facilities, except for a few restaurants, shut down. The streets are plowed but snow is several feet deep everywhere else.

Once the ice bridge forms between the island and mainland, crossings can be made by snowmobile. Inexperienced operators should not attempt the trip, and all travelers should be absolutely sure of ice and weather conditions. Or you can try **Great Lakes Air,** which flies between St. Ignace

Winter is the only time you're near an engine

and Mackinac. Call (906) 643-7165 for schedule and rates.

Snowmobiles are not allowed everywhere on the island. State Park regulations limit them to specified trails. There are, however, extensive opportunities for cross-country skiing and showshoeing.

You can also arrange in advance for a sleigh ride, at **Mackinac Island Carriage Tours.** (906) 847-3307. Seeing the island landmarks under their white mantle is an experience known by comparatively few, the sort of voyage that separates travelers from tourists.

In St. Ignace, there are three runs for downhill skiing and tubing at **Silver Mountain Ski Area.** In addition, 7 miles of crosscountry trails are on the property. It is west of town, at U.S. 2 and Cheeseman Road. (906) 643-8131. There is also ice skating at **Little Bear Arena,** on Marquette St., off N. State Street. (906) 643-8676.

The best cross-country skiing and snowmobiling in the Mackinaw City area is at Wilderness State Park. Sixteen miles of trails run across this 8,500-acre natural area.

KIDS

It's got horses and candy. So how can you beat Mackinac as a destination for children?

Some of the attractions are obvious. A trip in a horse-drawn carriage. The boat ride across. A mouthful of chocolate fudge. A tandem bike.

There are also pony rides at the **Chambers Riding Stable,** Market St. at Cadotte Ave. (906) 847-631.

The Haunted Theatre and Wax Museum is an altogether hokey attraction that sub-teens love because of the scary setting. It may be a little too scary for young children, though. It's right on Main Street in the middle of things.

There is a playground at **Mackinac Island Public School,** just west of downtown near the Boardwalk. A somewhat larger area, with skateboarding and volleyball facilities, as well as soccer and baseball fields, is located on Garrison Road, near Fort Holmes, at the high point of the island.

The Butterfly House, on McGulpin Street, is described in the Mackinac Walk section. A second display, Wings of Mackinac Butterfly Conservatory, is located at Surrey Hills, the island's carriage horse stables, behind the Grand Hotel.

AFTER DARK

Those who spend the night on the island, and don't especially like serenity, have plentiful opportunities to make some noise.

Best known of the live music venues is **Horn's Gaslight Bar,** with rock, reggae and blues every weekend in summer. The place also encourages college bands to perform, so Horn's attracts a young clientele who are there to boogie.

A slightly older crowd heads for the **Pink Pony,** in the Chippewa Hotel. This is famous as a boater's hangout, since it is just down from the marina. It is loud, the musicians are close to the customers and the banter between them is nonstop.

Patrick Sinclair's is named for the man who bought Mackinac from the Indians. With a name like that, what do you suppose is the prevailing musical style? The Irish and folkies prevail; except on Sundays, when the atmosphere is reggae and the dance floor comes alive.

Jamaica supplies a lot of the youthful summer help at island restaurants and hotels, and you can hear more sounds of that other island at the **French Outpost.** Steel drummers perform during the day, while at night the mood becomes rock oldies.

For some even older oldies, the Grand Hotel features big band ballroom specials in the **Terrace Room.** (Remember, you must wear a jacket and tie in the evening.)
   The Cupola Bar is quieter, with couples listening to piano or guitar music and gazing out at the night sky.

Casino

Kewadin Shores is located just north of St. Ignace, at 3039 Mackinac Trail (Old U.S. 2). There are 1,100 slots and a full assortment of table games in this Native American facility. The casino also operates a motor lodge with frontage on nearby Lake Huron. Call (800) 539-2346 for information and motel reservations.

ANNUAL EVENTS

February:

Mackinac Winterfest. A carnival of frozen frolics on the first weekend of the month. Events like a snowmobile scavenger hunt, snow golf and bowling and---everybody's favorite---the frozen fish toss. There is also entertainment, cross-country ski competitions and a human dogsled race.

Mackinaw Mush. A genuine sled dog race held annually since 1990 at Mackinaw City. It starts off with the blessing of the sleds, and then gathers steam with a variety of musical events and the race itself. Call (231) 436-MUSH for information.

May:

Memorial Day Celebration at Colonial Michilimackinac, Mackinaw City. Parades, food booths, 18th Century style military drills and music, all topped off by a re-enactment of the 1763 massacre. A bit macabre, perhaps, but good history lessons.

June:

Lilac Festival, Mackinac. One of the first things European settlers did when arriving in a new place was to plant lilac trees. It was a touch of home, a splash of springtime color in a strange land. Mackinac was no exception and lilacs have bloomed here since the 1780s. The festival only dates to 1949, but is still one of the oldest in the area. There are parades, decorated buggies, a golf tournament at the Grand Hotel, food booths. It runs for a week, usually in the second week of the month.

St. Ignace Car Show. One of the country's great gatherings of vintage automobiles and the people who collect them. It began in 1976 with a few hundred people. Now nearly 100,000 spectators make the trip across the Mackinac Bridge to observe the 2,500 participating cars, all of them dating from before 1980. Usually held on the third weekend of June.

July:

Fourth of July Celebration, Mackinac. A huge patriotic outburst, with fireworks, music, 38-gun salutes from the fort and the island's own unique sporting event, the stone skipping tournament.

Port Huron to Mackinac and Chicago to Mackinac Yacht Races. A shining spot on the boating calendar. The island jumps as the sailors make their way up the lakes and then party with dedication when they arrive. The Chicago race has been an annual event since 1907 (although the first one was held 8 years earlier) and the Port Huron race began in 1924.

August:

Battle Day Golf Tournament, Mackinac. Held on the 7th at Wawashkamo Golf Club, which was laid out over a War of 1812 battlefield.

Benjamin Blacksmith Convention, Mackinac. A tribute to the craft of the village smithy, with more than 20 of them giving demonstrations along Market Street. Held annually since 1985 on the first full weekend of the month.

September:

Jazz Weekend, Mackinac. Over Labor Day, the Grand Hotel hosts a number of jazz artists who perform in various settings around the island.

Around the Island Yacht Race. The culminating event of the boating season, as the boaters swing once around Mackinac for the prize.

Mackinac Bridge Walk. Traditionally led by the governor, this has become one of the State's most beloved traditions. It is the only time foot traffic is allowed on the bridge. Hordes of citizens follow in the footsteps of the chief executive to take in the view and the (usually) fine Labor Day weather.

October:

Oktoberfest. Beer and strudel and music in a traditional German harvest celebration on Mackinac.

Somewhere in Time Weekend. Fans of the cult film that starred the late Christopher Reeve and Jane Seymour flock to the island on the last weekend of the month to discuss fine points of the romantic fantasy and exchange memorabilia.

For complete information and exact dates for these events, contact the local tourist offices. Mackinac Island Chamber of Commerce: (800) 454-5227. Mackinaw Area Visitors Bureau: (800) 666-0160. St. Ignace Area Chamber of Commerce: (800) 338-6660.

HOSPITALS AND URGENT CARES

Mackinac Straits Hospital
200 Burdette Street, St. Ignace, MI 49781
(906) 643-8585

On the island; affiliated with the hospital,

Mackinac Island Medical Center
on Market Street, just north of Hoban
(906) 847-3582 or 911
Staffed all year